Hello Kitty & Her Friends Crafts Club

Hello Kitty
Tissue Paper
Activity Book

by Kris Hirschmann

Scholastic Inc.

New York Toronto London Auckland Sydney
Mexico City New Delhi Hong Kong Buenos Aires

Designer: Lee Kaplan
Illustrations: Yancey C. Labat
Photography: Rocco Melillo

ISBN 0-439-32841-1

12 11 10 9 8 7 6 5 4 3 2 1   2 3 4 5 6/0

Printed in the U.S.A.
First Scholastic printing, March 2002

Table of Contents

Get Ready for Tissue Paper Fun

Hello Kitty loves making crafts with tissue paper. So will you! That's because tissue paper is colorful, pretty, and easy to work with. Plus, there are so many great projects you can make with tissue paper.

Hello Kitty sometimes has a hard time deciding which project to do first, so her friend Rory is here to help her out. In this book, Hello Kitty and Rory share with you 17 of their favorite tissue paper projects. You can make these projects by yourself, or you can make these crafts with your friends!

Have fun!

Let's Get Started

With this book, you get twenty sheets of colorful tissue paper and three pairs of scissors (straight, wavy, and zigzag). There are also shapes printed in the back pages of this book. You can trace these shapes for some of the crafts or use them as examples of how to draw your own shapes.

Everything else you need for these crafts can be found around your house. Here's the list:

- Pencil
- Pen
- Felt-tip pen
- Ruler
- Glue
- Tape
- Construction paper
- Tracing paper
- Waxed paper

- Paper plate
- Hole punch
- Cotton balls
- String
- Disposable cup
- Paintbrush
- Cardboard paper-towel tube
- Paper towels

- Brown paper bag
- Flashlight
- Clean glass jar
- Box
- Tin can
- Blunt embroidery needle
- Food coloring

About Your Scissors:

There are three pairs of scissors in this kit. One pair has zigzag blades, one pair has curvy blades, and one has straight blades. Tissue paper is very thin and can tear easily, so when using your scissors, be sure to hold the paper tightly and cut carefully.

Your scissors are used to cut, but are also fun for making decorations or for putting finishing touches on your crafts. A few of the instructions in this book tell you how to use your special scissors, but mostly it's up to you. Use them whenever you want to make your finished crafts just a little bit more special!

Hello Kitty *in the* Garden

Hello Kitty loves the flowers, butterflies, and pretty ladybugs in her garden. Start your own tissue paper collection with the fun crafts in this section.

Pretty Rose:

Roses are a symbol of love. Help Hello Kitty make one of these beautiful buds for Rory!

What You Do:

1. Cut out a rectangular piece of tissue paper that is about 3" wide and 9" long in any color you like (this will be the color of your flower).

2. Fold ⅓ of the tissue paper length-wise.

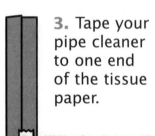

3. Tape your pipe cleaner to one end of the tissue paper.

4. Loosely roll the tissue paper around the pipe cleaner, pinching the bottom together as you roll to gather the base of the flower.

5. When you finish rolling, wrap a piece of tape around the bottom of the tissue paper to hold it in place.

6. To hide the tape, cut a small strip of green tissue paper, cover one side with glue, and wrap it around the bottom of your rosebud.

What You Need:

- **Ruler**
- **Scissors**
- **Tissue paper (any color)**
- **Green pipe cleaner**
- **Tape**
- **Glue**

HELLO KITTY SAYS

You can make a dozen beautiful roses in any color you like and give them to a special friend. Or you can wrap up a present for your friend with some tissue paper and tape a pretty rose on top of it. What a nice way to show friendship!

Easy Flower:

This flower is so easy to make, you can create a whole bouquet!

What You Do:

1. Cut out a rectangular piece of tissue paper that is about 3" wide and 9" long in any color you like (this will be the color of your flower).

2. Starting with a short edge, fold the tissue paper to look like an accordion (back and forth).

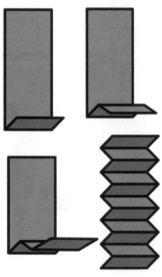

3. Take your pipe cleaner and bend it in half around the middle of the accordion-folded tissue paper. Pinch the middle of the pipe cleaner together so that it holds the tissue paper tight.

4. Starting just below the tissue paper, twist the two ends of the pipe cleaner together until you reach the bottom. This will make your flower stem.

5. Spread a line of glue on the tissue paper, as shown in the picture.

6. Pull the sides of the folded tissue paper toward each other. Pinch them together to glue them.

7. Repeat steps 5 and 6 on the other side of the folded tissue paper.

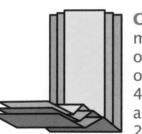

Colorful flower: You can also make this craft using several colors of tissue paper, instead of one. Cut one piece of paper that measures 4"x12", one that measures 3"x12", and one that measures 2"x12". Lay the strips on one another, as shown in the picture, then follow the same steps you used to make a single-color flower.

What You Need:

- **Ruler**
- **Scissors**
- **Tissue paper (any color)**
- **Green pipe cleaner**
- **Glue**

❋ Hint: Be sure when you bend the pipe cleaner over your flower that the multicolored side is facing up.

HELLo KiTTY SAYS Make lots of flowers and give them to all of your friends!

Cute Ladybug:

Hello Kitty and Rory think ladybugs are cute—and they keep many harmful bugs away. Make a ladybug or two to protect your own garden!

What You Do:

1. Trace the ladybug shape from page 38 onto a piece of black construction paper and cut it out. This will make your ladybug's legs and antennae. Set the shape aside.

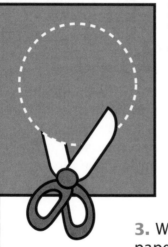

2. Cut out a circle of red tissue paper that is about 4" across.

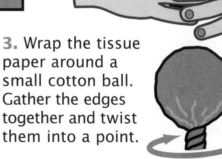

What You Need:

- Pencil
- Black construction paper
- Scissors
- Tissue paper (red and black)
- Ruler
- Cotton ball
- Glue

3. Wrap the tissue paper around a small cotton ball. Gather the edges together and twist them into a point.

8

4. Spread some glue onto the center of the black shape you cut out in step 1.

5. Then, poke the twisted part of the red tissue paper through the hole in the black shape. Glue it in place.

6. Trim off the point on the red tissue paper so your ladybug can sit flat.

7. Cut out some small dots from your black tissue paper. Glue them to your ladybug's body.

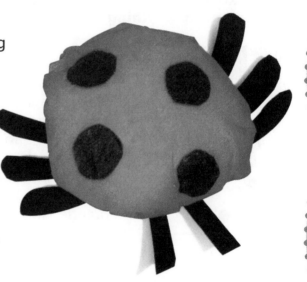

HELLO KITTY SAYS

Hold a ladybug in your hand, make a wish, and then gently blow so she flies away. The ladybug will take your wish along with her!

Perfect Pictures

You can use colored tissue paper to make all kinds of neat pictures.
Here are a few of Hello Kitty and Rory's favorites!

Sunburst Hello Kitty Mosaic:

**A mosaic is a picture made out of lots and lots of little pieces.
You can make anything—even a picture of Hello Kitty!**

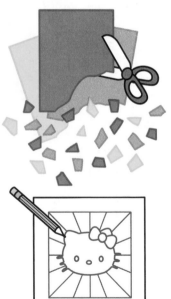

What You Do:

1. Cut up lots of little pieces of tissue paper. Make the pieces all different shapes and sizes. You'll need red, black, and yellow tissue paper to make Hello Kitty's face and head. You can use any colors you want for the sunburst background and the border. Yellow, orange, and blue are pretty.

2. Trace the Hello Kitty pattern from page 39 onto a piece of white paper.

What You Need:

- Scissors
- Tissue paper (red, yellow, and black, plus other colors of your choice)
- White paper
- Tape
- Glue
- Pencil

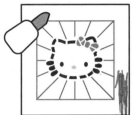 **3.** Glue the red tissue paper pieces onto Hello Kitty's bow, the black ones onto the border of her face and her eyes, and the yellow one onto her nose.

 **4.** Glue on the yellow and orange pieces of tissue paper to make the sunburst background. Leave some space (about 1") around your picture so that you can make a border.

 **5.** When you're finished filling in the pattern, add a border to your picture. You can make a border out of just a few long strips of tissue paper or you can make it out of many small pieces. It's up to you.

 **6.** Use your wavy or zigzag scissors to cut around the edges of your finished mosaic for a jazzy frame!

HELLO KITTY SAYS

You can also make a mosaic using Rory's picture on page 40 as a guide. Or can you make a picture of yourself into a mosaic?

Underwater Tissue Paper Collage:

Collages are fun and easy to do. Hello Kitty and Rory like to make underwater scenes. See if you like creating the deep blue sea, too.

What You Do:

1. Cut out wavy strips of blue tissue paper to make waves for your underwater scene. Use your glue to attach the waves to your paper plate.

2. To make a sandy bottom, cut out a piece of yellow tissue paper. Glue it to the bottom of the plate.

3. To make seaweed, cut out pieces of light and dark green tissue paper. Glue them to the plate, wherever you think they look best.

What You Need:

- Scissors
- Tissue paper (various colors)
- Glue
- Paper plate
- Hole punch
- String

12

4. Cut out fish of several sizes in any color of tissue paper you like. Glue them to the plate wherever you want. You can make scales and eyes for the fish by adding little pieces of tissue paper, as shown.

5. If you'd like to make a starfish, cut out a piece of tissue paper in a star shape and glue it to the sandy bottom.

6. Punch a hole in the top of the paper plate. Tie a string loop through the hole so you can hang your creation!

HELLO KITTY SAYS

13

Maybe you could make a collage that shows some of your favorite things. Wouldn't that be fun?

"Coloring" with Tissue Paper:

You can "color" anything using this fun technique. It takes a while to do, but it's easy and the results are really neat. Hold still, Rory! I'm going to "color" a picture of your face!

What You Do:

1. Trace the pattern of Rory's head on page 40 onto a sheet of white paper.

2. Cut lots of little squares of black tissue paper. Each square should be about 1"x1", but exact measurements aren't necessary. These will be used to form the outline of Rory's head.

What You Need:

- Scissors
- Tissue paper (black, yellow, white, and red)
- Ruler
- White paper
- Glue
- Waxed paper
- Pencil with an eraser end

3. Put a little pool of white glue on a piece of waxed paper.

4. Crinkle a black tissue paper square around the eraser end of a pencil to make a cup shape, and dip it into the white glue. Then, press the cup onto the white paper. Follow the outlines of Rory's head pattern to see where to put the black cups. Continue gluing black cups until you've covered all of the black outlines, as well as Rory's eyes and mouth.

5. Cut out and glue on lots of little yellow squares of tissue paper to give Rory a yellow face. Add a white muzzle and a red nose.

6. When you've finished "coloring" in all of Rory's face, use your zigzag or wavy scissors to cut around the edges of the white paper of your picture to create a neat frame for him.

15

Light-catcher Crafts

One of the best things about tissue paper is the way it catches the light. Why not make some great shine-through crafts with Hello Kitty and Rory?

Hello Kitty Lamp Hanger:

Rory has a cool stained-glass craft that looks just like his friend Hello Kitty. He hangs it near his lamp where he can see it every night. It reminds him of his special friendship with Hello Kitty!

What You Need:

- Pencil
- White tracing paper
- Pen
- Black construction paper
- Scissors
- Craft knife
- Glue
- Tissue paper (red, white, yellow, and blue)
- String
- Tape

What You Do:

1. Trace the Hello Kitty shape from page 41 onto a piece of white tracing paper.

2. Set the white tracing paper onto a piece of black construction paper Draw over the lines of the pattern with a pen. Press hard enough so that you leave dents in the black paper underneath.

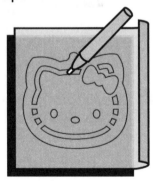

3. Cut along the dents you left in the black paper. (Ask a grown-up to cut out the holes for Hello Kitty's eyes and nose with a craft knife.)

Back

Front

4. Lay the black paper on a table with the bow on the left side. Spread a little glue around the edges of each cutout hole. Then stick tissue paper over the holes. Put red tissue paper over Hello Kitty's bow, white tissue paper over Hello Kitty's eyes, yellow tissue paper over Hello Kitty's nose, and blue tissue paper all around Hello Kitty's face.

5. Flip the cutout over and poke a hole through the bump at the top of the lamp hanger, as shown.

6. Tie a loop of string through the hole. Use a little piece of tape to attach the loop to the edge of a lampshade. Turn on the lamp and enjoy the colors!

HELLO KITTY SAYS

What a *bright* idea! Why not try to make a lamp hanger that looks like Rory, too?

Rainbow Window Cling:

Hello Kitty and Rory like to make these super rainbows, then stick them on their windows. You can, too.

What You Do:

1. Make a mixture of white glue and water in a disposable cup. You should use about half glue and half water.

2. Set a piece of waxed paper (about 13"x12") on a flat work surface.

3. Cut long, thin strips of tissue paper (about 12"x¾") in these seven colors: red, orange, yellow, green, blue, light blue, purple.

What You Need:

- **Glue**
- **Water**
- **Disposable cup**
- **Waxed paper**
- **Ruler**
- **Scissors**
- **Tissue paper (red, orange, yellow, green, blue, light blue, and purple)**
- **Paintbrush**
- **White paper**
- **Cotton balls**
- **Tape**

4. Lay the purple strip on the waxed paper. Use a paintbrush to soak the purple strip with the glue-and-water mixture.

5. Repeat step 4 with the rest of the strips in this order: light blue above the purple, then blue, green, yellow, orange, and red. (You can use the picture on this page as a guide.)

6. When all the tissue paper strips are glued on, let them dry completely. Then, use scissors to cut them out in a rainbow shape.

7. Here's how to make the clouds for your rainbow. First, use your scissors to cut two nice, puffy cloud shapes about 4½"x7" out of white paper. Glue these to the bottoms of your rainbow, on the back (waxed paper side).

8. Gently pull a few cotton balls to billow them out, then glue them to the front of your paper clouds.

9. Make two small tape loops and stick them to the back of the rainbow. Now you can stick your rainbow onto your window.

HELLO KITTY SAYS
What else can you make besides rainbows? Flowers and butterflies make pretty window clings, too!

Nifty Night-lights:

Hello Kitty and Rory like to make these nifty night-lights during their sleepovers!

What You Do:

1. Trace the Hello Kitty head shape from page 42 onto a piece of white 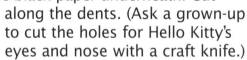 tracing paper. To make other night-lights, you can also trace the heart and flower shapes from page 42.

2. Set the white tracing paper on a piece of black construction paper. Draw over the lines with a pen. Press hard enough so that you leave dents in the black paper underneath. Cut along the dents. (Ask a grown-up to cut the holes for Hello Kitty's eyes and nose with a craft knife.)

What You Need:

- **Pencil**
- **White tracing paper**
- **Pen**
- **Black construction paper**
- **Scissors**
- **Craft knife**
- **Ruler**
- **Glue**
- **Tissue paper (three colors)**
- **Flashlight**

3. Trace the night-light frame from page 42 onto a piece of white tracing paper. Set the white paper on a piece of black construction paper and draw over the lines with a pen, just like you did in step 2. If you're making more than one night-light, repeat this process on different parts of the construction paper. Cut out your frame or frames using the dents as guides.

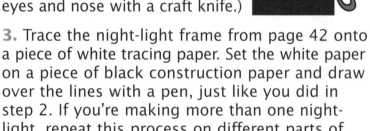

4. Cut a piece of tissue paper, 2¾" x 2¾", in any color you'd like (use different colors if you've made extra frames). Spread glue around the edges of the square hole in each frame. Then stick the square of tissue paper over the hole.

5. Flip the frame over so the raggedy edges of the tissue paper are underneath. Glue the shapes you cut out in step 2 to the tissue paper in each frame.

6. Bend back the edges of the frame so that it can stand up.

7. Turn on a flashlight and set your night-light frame in front of it. If you made more than one frame, simply change it whenever you want a new night-light!

HELLO KITTY SAYS

The dark is never scary when you are surrounded by friends!

Special Stuff...Shhh!!

Hello Kitty and Rory love to keep special stuff—
and to make neat places to keep them in.

Jazzy Jar:

**Hello Kitty and Rory turn old glass jars into cool containers.
Now they want to share their discovery with you!**

What You Do:

1. Make a mixture of white glue and water in a disposable cup. You should use about half glue and half water.

2. Cut out a piece of tissue paper that's just a bit wider than the jar you've chosen, and is long enough to wrap around it.

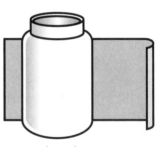

3. Cut a bunch of shapes out of different colors of tissue paper. You can make hearts, flowers, stars, or anything else you like.

What You Need:
- **Glue**
- **Water**
- **Disposable cup**
- **Tissue paper (several colors)**
- **Scissors**
- **Clean glass jar**
- **Paintbrush**

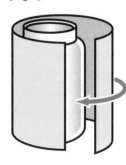

4. Wrap the tissue paper you cut in step 2 around the jar. Then use the paintbrush to soak the tissue paper with the glue-and-water mixture. The tissue paper will stick to the jar.

5. While the tissue paper is still wet, press the shapes you cut in step 3 all over the jar in any pattern you like. After you press each shape to the jar, use the paintbrush to soak it with the glue-and-water mixture.

6. Use your scissors to trim any loose tissue paper near the mouth of the jar.

7. Put the jar in a safe place where it can dry for a couple of hours. When it's completely dry, it's ready to use!

HELLO KITTY SAYS

I'm going to use my special jar to store some candy. Rory says he's using his for saving pennies. What are you using yours for?

Tiny Basket:

Hello Kitty and Rory think that tiny baskets are perfect for holding tiny things. What will you put in your basket?

What You Do:

1. Trace the basket shape from page 43 onto a piece of white paper.

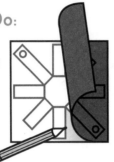

2. Glue a piece of tissue paper, in any color you like, over the shape, completely covering it, and let it dry.

3. Cut out the basket shape and poke holes in the two long spokes, using your scissors or a hole punch.

4. Bend up all of the spokes so that the tissue paper is on the outside.

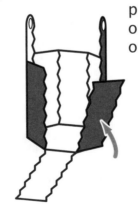

5. Cut three long, thin strips of tissue paper, each about ½" wide and 7½" long. Use a different color from the one you used to cover the basket shape.

What You Need:

- **White paper**
- **Pencil**
- **Glue**
- **Tissue paper (two colors)**
- **Scissors**
- **Hole punch (optional)**
- **Ruler**
- **String**

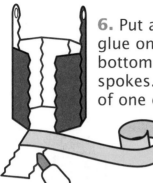

6. Put a little dab of glue on the inside bottom of one of the spokes. Stick one end of one of the tissue paper strips to the glue.

7. Weave the strip in and out of the spokes until you get back to where you started. Gently pull the strip tight and glue it to secure.

8. Put another dab of glue on a different spoke above the first strip of tissue paper, and begin weaving the second strip as you did the first one in step 7. This time, however, be sure to weave outside the strips that you weaved inside with the first strip. This way, all the spokes will stand up straight.

9. Weave your third strip in the same way, weaving outside those spokes that you weaved inside with your second strip of tissue paper.

Tie a string through the holes in the two long spokes to create a handle.

Crinkle Box:

Hello Kitty keeps her treasures in a special crinkle box that she made herself. She likes her box so much that she made one for Rory, too!

What You Do:

1. Paint over an old box with white paint to cover up any words or pictures. Set the box aside and let it dry completely.

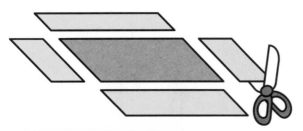

2. Cut separate pieces of tissue paper to cover each side of the box, as well as the lid. (You can use all one color or many different colors.) Each piece should be a little bigger than the area it will cover.

3. Make a mixture of white glue and water in a disposable cup. You should use about half glue and half water.

4. Scrunch up a piece of tissue paper, then open it back up.

5. Lay the crinkled piece of tissue paper over the box panel you want to cover. Use a paintbrush to soak the paper with the glue-and-water mixture. You can push the damp paper around the box to make it really wrinkly if you want, but be gentle so the tissue paper doesn't rip.

6. Repeat steps 4 and 5 with the other sides of the box and the lid.

7. Cut out some shapes to stick to your box with the glue-and-water mixture. They can be anything you like—hearts, stars, flowers, or pictures of Hello Kitty and Rory!

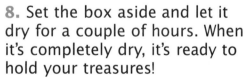

8. Set the box aside and let it dry for a couple of hours. When it's completely dry, it's ready to hold your treasures!

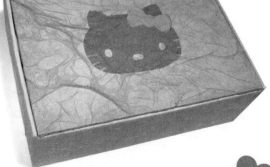

HELLO KITTY SAYS

Rory loved the crinkle box I made for him. I bet your friends will love crinkle boxes of their own, too!

The Prettiest Presents

Giving gifts to your friends is a lot of fun. And it's even more fun when the gifts are "dressed up" with fancy paper and tags! Hello Kitty and Rory show you how.

Tie-dyed Paper:

Tissue paper makes great gift-wrapping paper—especially when it's tie-dyed! Hello Kitty and Rory sometimes dye the tissue paper in fun, funky colors to make it extra cool.

What You Do:

1. Put a few drops of food coloring into a disposable cup. Add a little water to make the "dye." Repeat with as many cups and colors as you like to make several batches of dye.

What You Need:

- **Food coloring**
- **Disposable cups**
- **Water**
- **Scissors**
- **Tissue paper (any light color)**
- **Paper towels**
- **Paintbrush**

2. Cut a piece of tissue paper (light colors work best) into any size and shape you want.

3. Fold the tissue paper into a small packet. Fold it any way you want.

4. Quickly dip a corner of the tissue paper packet into a dye cup. Repeat with different corners and different colors of dye.

5. When you have done as much dying as you want, press the tissue paper packet between two paper towels to get rid of extra moisture.

6. Unfold the packet very slowly and carefully so you don't rip it. Lay the tie-dyed sheet of tissue paper on a paper towel and let it dry.

Other Techniques

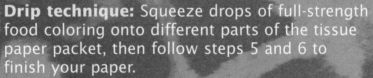

Brush technique: Use a paintbrush to paint each folded edge with dye, then follow steps 5 and 6 to finish your paper.

Drip technique: Squeeze drops of full-strength food coloring onto different parts of the tissue paper packet, then follow steps 5 and 6 to finish your paper.

To make a pretty surprise package, put a few candies or another small gift in the middle of your tissue paper. Then gather the edges and tie the package closed with a little piece of ribbon.

Terrific Tags:

Hello Kitty and Rory know that a gift isn't complete until it carries a special note from a special friend!

What You Do:

1. Trace the Hello Kitty head, heart, and flower shapes from page 38 onto a piece of white tracing paper.

2. Set the white tracing paper on a piece of thin cardboard. Draw over the lines with a pen. Press hard enough so that you'll leave dents in the cardboard.

What You Need:

- **White tracing paper**
- **Pen**
- **Thin cardboard, like a file folder**
- **Tissue paper (three colors)**
- **Glue**
- **Water**
- **Disposable cup**
- **Paintbrush**
- **Scissors**
- **Ruler**
- **Brown paper bag**
- **Hole punch**

3. Scrunch up a piece of tissue paper and then open it back up. Create a mixture of glue and water in a small paper cup. You should use about half glue and half water. Place the crinkled paper over one of the tracings on your cardboard. Spread the glue-and-water mixture over the paper to glue it in place. Put the cardboard aside until the tissue paper is completely dry.

4. Cut out the shape using the dents as a guide.

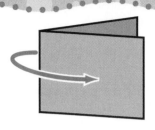

5. Cut a rectangular piece out of a brown paper bag measuring about 2½" wide and 6" long. Fold in half.

6. Use your glue to attach the shape you made to the brown paper tag.

7. Punch a hole in the upper left-hand corner of the tag using a hole punch.

8. Cut a long, thin piece of tissue paper. Twist gently but firmly to make paper string.

9. Put a paper string through the hole in the tag. Use the string to tie the tag to a gift!

10. Repeat with the other two shapes using different colors of tissue paper.

HELLo KiTTY SAYS

Inside my gift tag, I'm going to write:
Dear Rory, you are a great friend!
Love, Hello Kitty.

Pretty Package:

Hello Kitty thinks that a friend like Rory deserves a unique package. So she invented a neat way to wrap small gifts.

What You Do:

1. Lay a paper-towel tube on a sheet of tissue paper. Cut the tissue paper into a long strip that's about the same width as the cardboard tube.

2. Cut the tube into three pieces of about the same length. Put a little gift into one of the tubes.

3. Lay the tubes on the tissue paper, as shown, with the gift tube in the middle. Use your glue to attach only the middle tube to the tissue paper.

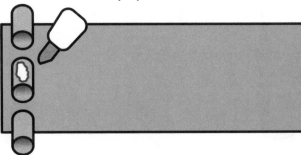

What You Need:

- **Cardboard paper towel tube**
- **Tissue paper (any color)**
- **Scissors**
- **Glue**
- **Ribbon**

4. Roll the tubes forward until you have rolled up the entire tissue paper strip. Use your glue to seal the tissue paper.

5. Cut a piece of ribbon and put it around the tissue paper on one side of the middle gift tube. Tie a single knot in the ribbon and carefully pull it tight to squeeze the tissue paper shut. Tie another knot and finish with a bow.

6. Tie a second piece of ribbon on the other side of the middle gift tube. Remove both of the end tubes.

7. Cut out any shapes you'd like from your tissue paper and glue them to your finished package for decoration.

HELLO KITTY SAYS

I can never decide which is better—getting gifts, or giving them. Both are so much fun!

Hello Kitty's *Best-ever* Party Crafts

Everyone loves a party, especially Hello Kitty! She and Rory even like to make their own party crafts and decorations. Follow these easy steps and you can, too!

Fun Banners:

Hello Kitty and Rory learned in school that tissue paper banners are a Mexican party favorite. In Mexico, this craft is called *papel picado*, which means "pierced paper."

What You Do:

1. Cut out a rectangular piece of tissue paper that is about 6" wide and 8" long.

2. Fold the paper in half. Fold it in half three more times until you have a folded packet measuring about 1½"x2".

What You Need:

- **Ruler**
- **Scissors**
- **Tissue paper (several colors)**
- **String**
- **Tape**

3. Use your scissors to snip mini shapes out of the tissue paper packet. Don't cut all the way across the packet. If you do, it will fall apart!

4. Carefully open the tissue paper packet and spread it flat.

5. Repeat steps 1 through 4 to make as many cutout sheets as you like.

6. Lay all the sheets you've just made next to one another. Then lay a string across the top of the sheets, about 1" down from the top.

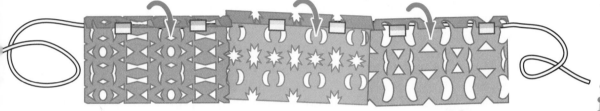

7. Fold the tops of the sheets down over the string and use your tape to close them.

Now hang your fun banners in your room and invite some friends over for a party!

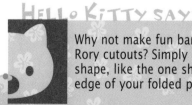

HELLO KiTTY SAYS

Why not make fun banners with Rory cutouts? Simply cut out a shape, like the one shown, on any edge of your folded packet!

Hawaiian Lei:

In Hawaii, leis stand for "love" and "welcome." Sometimes Hello Kitty and Rory exchange this sweet message with homemade tissue paper leis!

What You Do:

1. Trace around the bottom of an aluminum can onto different colors of tissue paper. You need about 50 tissue paper circles to make a good lei. Cut out all the circles.

2. Thread a long piece of string through a blunt embroidery needle. The string should be about 3 feet long. Tie a loose knot at the other end of the string, leaving about 4" below the knot.

What You Need:

- Pencil
- Aluminum can
- Tissue paper (many colors)
- Scissors
- String
- Embroidery needle
- Ruler

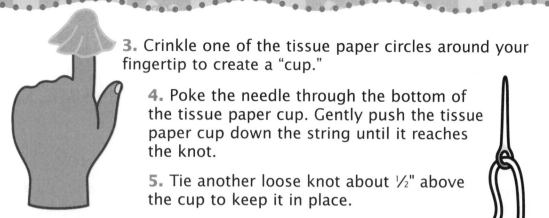

3. Crinkle one of the tissue paper circles around your fingertip to create a "cup."

4. Poke the needle through the bottom of the tissue paper cup. Gently push the tissue paper cup down the string until it reaches the knot.

5. Tie another loose knot about ½" above the cup to keep it in place.

6. Repeat steps 3 through 5 until you're happy with the length of your lei.

Tie a double knot with the two ends of the string to finish your lei. Trim off any extra string.

HELLO KITTY SAYS

In Hawaii, it's traditional to give a kiss on the cheek along with a lei.

Hello Kitty Shapes to Trace

To Trace a Shape:

Get some thin white paper that is easy to see through. (This is called white tracing paper in the instructions.) Place the paper on the shape you want to trace and draw on top of all the lines. When you're done, you will have a handmade copy of the shape!

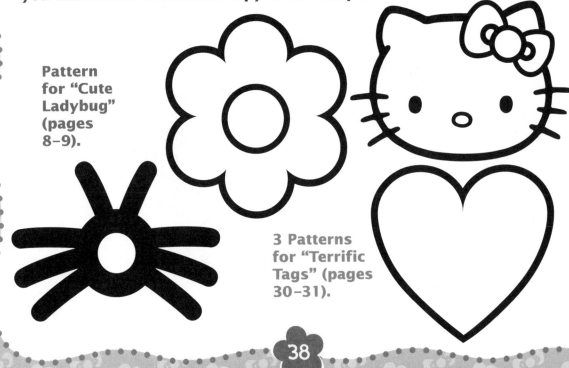

Pattern for "Cute Ladybug" (pages 8–9).

3 Patterns for "Terrific Tags" (pages 30–31).

Pattern for "Sunburst Hello Kitty Mosaic" (pages 10–11).

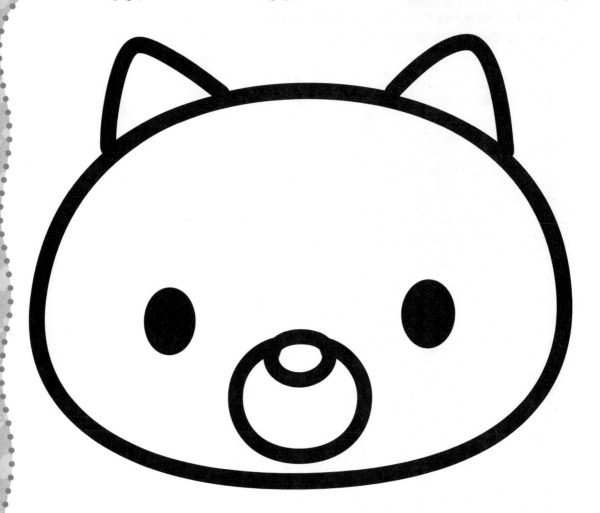

Pattern for " 'Coloring' with Tissue Paper" (pages 14–15).

Pattern for "Hello Kitty Lamp Hanger" (pages 16–17).

4 Patterns for "Nifty Night-lights" (pages 20–21).

Pattern for "Tiny Basket"
(pages 24–25).

See Ya, say Hello Kitty and Rory

Hello Kitty and Rory think tissue paper crafts are super for two reasons. First, they are lots of fun to make. And second, they look fabulous when they're done. Hello Kitty always feels very proud of herself when she finishes a beautiful tissue paper craft, and she wants you to have that same great feeling!

Hello Kitty and Rory sure hope you liked doing all of their favorite tissue paper crafts. Till next time!

Love,

xoxox Hello Kitty and Rory

44